HIGH FASHION

OUT OF THIS WORLD!

by Lisa Moore

SCHOOL PUBLISHERS

Cover, ©NASA; p.3, ©NASA/Langley Research Center; p.4, ©AP/Wide World Photo p.5, ©U.S. Air Force; p.6, ©NASA/Langley Research Center; p.7–8, ©NASA; p.10, ©NASA/Kennedy Space Center; p.11, ©NASA; p.12, ©CORBIS; p.13, ©StockTrek/PhotoDisc; p.14, ©Roger Ressmeyer/CORBIS.

Requests for permission to make copies of any part of the work should be addressed to School Permissions and Copyrights, Harcourt, Inc., 6277 Sea Harbor Drive, Orlando, Florida 32887–6777. Fax: 407-345-2418.

HARCOURT and the Harcourt Logo are trademarks of Harcourt, Inc., registered in the United States of America and/or other jurisdictions.

Printed in China

ISBN 10:   0-15-377436-3
ISBN 13:   978-0-15-377436-2

Ordering Options
ISBN 10:   0-15-377149-6 (Grade 5 Collection)
ISBN 13:   978-0-15-377149-1 (Grade 5 Collection)
ISBN 10:   0-15-377897-0 (package of 5)
ISBN 13:   978-0-15-377897-1 (package of 5)

2 3 4 5 6 7 8 9 10   0940   17 16 15 14 13 12 11 10 09

What if?

What would happen if you stepped on the moon but forgot your space suit? It wouldn't be pretty. Consider this:

- With no oxygen to breathe, you would pass out in fifteen seconds.
- With no air pressure, your blood would "boil" and then freeze.
- You could face heat of 248° Fahrenheit (120°C)!
- You could face cold of -148° Fahrenheit (-100°C)!
- You would be exposed to high levels of radiation.
- You would be hit by pieces of dust or rock moving at high speeds.

How's that for dangerous? As soon as scientists began to imagine people in space, they knew they would have to invent some protection that was out of this world: the space suit. Like many things, space suits have changed over time. They started out simple and have become more and more complex over the years.

The First Space Suit

Wiley Post was a pilot long before astronauts were sent into space. He was born in 1898, in Grand Saline, Texas. In 1926, he bought his first airplane. He set two world records for flying around the world. In July 1931, he flew around the world in eight days and sixteen hours with another person. In July 1933, he did it in seven days, nineteen hours—alone. In addition, Post flew a series of high-altitude research flights, wearing a suit he helped design himself. He was one of the first humans ever to fly in space.

Wiley Post was very daring. To protect himself from the dangers one encounters when one reaches high altitudes, a specially designed space suit was made for Post. It was made of rubberized fabric, leather gloves, rubber boots, and an aluminum helmet. Post made ten flights in this suit. He died when his plane crashed and ignited near Point Barrow, Alaska, in 1935.

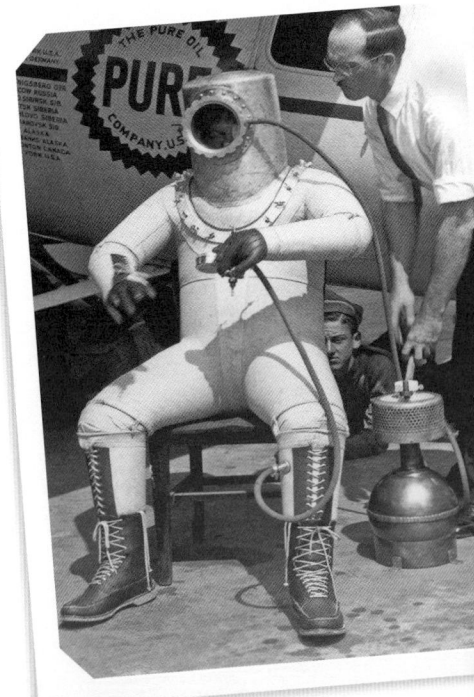

Pushing the Limits

During the middle of the twentieth century, test pilots and bomber pilots pushed the limits of altitude and speed. They tried to see how fast and how high they could go in a plane. To do so, the pilots needed special suits.

The United States Navy had suits made for pilots during World War II. The suits protected the pilots when they flew pressurized planes if the pressure failed.

After World War II, many American businesses wanted to make and supply products for the military. One chemical company made twenty new "space-age materials" and sold these materials to the military so that better and safer suits, gloves, helmets, and boots could be made for pilots. Over the years, zippers and laces were added to the suits. Changes at the elbows, knees, and shoulders allowed greater movement. Suits grew lighter and stronger and could be individually sized.

The First Suits in Space

By the 1960s, the United States was planning a trip to outer space for the first time. President John F. Kennedy had set the goal of putting a person on the moon before 1970. Project Mercury was America's first step toward that goal of landing on the moon.

The goals of Project Mercury were (1) to have a person orbit the earth in a spacecraft, (2) to recover the spacecraft safely, and (3) to learn about working in space. There were six Mercury missions from 1961 through 1963.

The Mercury astronauts traveled alone in the silence and tranquility of space. Their suits had inner layers of rubber-coated nylon and outer layers of metallic cloth. As before, the suits were only pressurized if the cabin pressure failed. Fortunately, none of the flights needed this backup.

Two Suits for Two Men

The second United States space program began in 1962. It was called Gemini because two astronauts went on each flight, and Gemini is a constellation with twin stars. The goals were (1) to have astronauts pilot longer flights, (2) to dock with, or hook up to, other things in space, and (3) to land at a specific place. The Gemini missions included space walks. In order to walk in space, astronauts needed fully pressurized suits that would protect them from the dangers listed earlier.

The Gemini suits had several layers. The inside layer was a human-shaped artificial rubber bag covered by netting. Over this was a layer of tough material to protect the wearer from bumps and scrapes. Air came into the suit through a tube connected to the spaceship. During the Gemini program, the astronauts had some problems with their suits. They often overheated. Also, the helmets fogged up, leaving astronauts squinting to see. These problems would be solved before the next phase of America's space program: Apollo.

Armored for the Moon

The goal of the Apollo program was simply stated: to land astronauts on the surface of the moon. Each Apollo mission needed fifteen space suits—and there were twelve missions. Each of the three astronauts had a training suit, a flight suit, and a backup flight suit. There were three backup astronauts, and they each had one training suit and one flight suit. Each suit was made especially for the astronaut who wore it. None were used more than once. That's a lot of suits to use only once!

Apollo suits marked a big improvement in space suit design. Various features were added to the space suits that were used for walking on the moon. Communication was possible between astronauts since the helmets muffled sounds. There were a pair of over boots, gloves with rubber fingers, a set of filters worn over the helmet for protection from the sun, and a backpack with air and cooling systems. The space suit and backpack weighed 180 pounds (82 kg) in the earth's gravity. In the moon's gravity, they only weighed 30 pounds (14 kg).

The space suit used to walk on the moon looked like this.

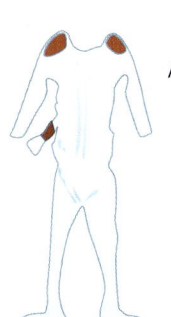

Liquid Cooling and Ventilation Garment

Arm Assembly

Hard Upper Torso

Helmet/ Extravehicular Visor Assembly

Communications Carrier Assembly

Display and Control Module

Airlock Adapter Plate

EMU Electrical Harness

Primary Life Support Subsystem

Gloves

Secondary Oxygen Pack

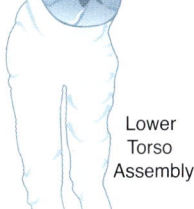

Lower Torso Assembly

Service and Cooling Umbilical

In-suit Drink Bag

Contaminant Control Cartridge

Battery

Shuttle Suits

As of 1981, the United States began to use space shuttles to carry astronauts into space. These huge orbiters carried five to seven astronauts. Unlike spacecrafts that were jettisoned after use, shuttles returned after a flight and could make additional flights. There were only six space shuttles. They flew more than one hundred missions in about 25 years. Only two were unsuccessful during that time.

A group of about 120 astronauts crewed the space shuttles. Space suits were worn only during liftoff and reentry. The rest of the time in space, astronauts wore normal clothes. The suits were made of many interchangeable parts to fit different sizes and shapes of people. Unlike Apollo suits, shuttle suits lasted up to fifteen years and served many missions.

Challenger crew

On January 28, 1986, Americans watched the space shuttle *Challenger* blast off. Many people watched because a teacher was onboard. Seventy-three seconds into the mission, the *Challenger* exploded, killing everyone onboard.

Today, in light of the *Challenger* tragedy, all space shuttle astronauts wear pressurized suits during takeoff and reentry. These suits are designed for emergencies, with parachutes and inflatable life preservers. These special suits may not have saved the lives of the seven people aboard the *Challenger*, but they may save lives in the future.

What Is an EMU?

If you think an emu is a kind of bird, you are not wrong. An EMU, however, is also a reusable suit made for working outside in space. The letters EMU stand for Extravehicular Mobility Unit. Like shuttle suits, EMUs are built from pieces that can be fitted together in different ways for different astronauts. Like the shuttle suits—and the shuttles—EMUs are used more than once.

An EMU is self-contained, which means that it does not depend on support from a spacecraft. EMUs have hard torsos that carry their own life-support systems, including oxygen, water, and temperature and air pressure controls. Astronauts can work outside in space in EMUs for several hours at a time. These astronauts must be very brave, don't you think?

Space-walk Checklist

Imagine that you are going to take a space walk.
Here are all the things you have to do to get ready.
Just a few easy steps!

- Breathe pure 100% oxygen for 30 minutes.
- Put on the first layer of your space suit.
- Attach communication equipment to your EMU.
- Attach life-support system to your EMU.
- Attach arms to your EMU.
- Rub your visor with antifog goo.
- Attach a mirror and checklist to your sleeves.
- Put a food bar and drink bag inside your EMU.
- Check the lights and cameras to make sure they work.
- Place the visor on your helmet.
- Connect and check your communications equipment.
- Step into the lower part of your EMU.
- Plug your support system controls into the spacecraft.
- Wiggle into the upper-torso part of your EMU.
- Attach the cooling tubes of your EMU to the life-support system.
- Attach the electricity to your life-support system.
- Lock the lower part of the EMU to the upper part.
- Put on the helmet.
- Put on your interior comfort gloves.
- Lock your visor to your helmet.
- Lock on your outer gloves.
- Check your EMU for leaks.
- Open the outer airlock door.

"High Fashion" in the Future

What will space suits look like in 2100? In 2500? What do you think? For missions taking people to places like Mars, NASA scientists are working on hard suits that offer more durable protection. However, they must be more flexible; the Apollo astronauts felt limited and cramped. The suits must weigh less than the EMUs since there is some gravity on Mars. The EMUs are weightless in space where there is zero gravity, so it doesn't matter if they are heavy there.

Who knows? Maybe you'll grow up to design space suits. At $12 million apiece, you potentially couldn't choose a more successful fashion career!

Think Critically

1. Why do astronauts need to wear space suits?

2. Name ways in which the Apollo space suits were different from the Mercury space suits.

3. One sentence on page 4 expresses an opinion. Which sentence is it?

4. Write one fact about this book. Then write one opinion.

5. Does this book make you want to travel into space? Why or why not?

 **Science**

Be a High Fashion Designer Imagine that you have been hired to design a space suit for astronauts who will walk on the surface of Mars in 2500. Use what you've learned from this book to design a space suit that will meet their needs. You may need to find out more about Mars before you begin.

School-Home Connection Survey your friends and family about the kinds of protective clothing they own. From what kinds of natural forces do they need protection? What other kinds of protective gear do they use (sunscreen, mosquito netting, umbrellas, etc.)? List as many examples as you can.

Word Count: 1,595 (with graphic 1,657)

ALTITUDE!

by Lisa Moore
illustrated by Rob Kneebone

Harcourt
SCHOOL PUBLISHERS

Cover, ©PhotoDisc/Punch Stock; p.4, ©Ingram Publishing SuperStock; p.10, ©David Young-Wolff/PhotoEdit; p.12, ©Galen Rowell/CORBIS; p.15, ©David Samuel Robbins/CORBIS.

Printed in China

ISBN 10: 0-15-380477-7
ISBN 13: 978-0-15-380477-9

Ordering Options
ISBN 10: 0-15-377149-6 (Grade 5 Collection)
ISBN 13: 978-0-15-377149-1 (Grade 5 Collection)
ISBN 10: 0-15-380687-7 (package of 5)
ISBN 13: 978-0-15-380687-2 (package of 5)

2 3 4 5 6 7 8 9 10 0940 17 16 15 14 13 12 11 10 09